COSTUME, TRADITION, AND CULTURE:
REFLECTING ON THE PAST

Musical Instruments from Around the World

by

Judy L. Hasday

Chelsea House Publishers
Philadelphia

To Eleanor Hasday Klein, with love

CHELSEA HOUSE PUBLISHERS
Editor-in-Chief Stephen Reginald
Managing Editor James D. Gallagher
Production Manager Pamela Loos
Art Director Sara Davis
Picture Editor Judy Hasday
Senior Production Editor Lisa Chippendale
Designer Takeshi Takahashi

First Printing

1 3 5 7 9 8 6 4 2

Library of Congress Cataloging-in-Publication Data

Hasday, Judy L.
Musical instruments from around the world / by
Judy L. Hasday.

  p. cm. — (Costume, tradition, and culture: reflecting on
the past)
Includes bibliographical references (p.) and index.
Summary: Highlights twenty-five musical instruments from
around the world, arranged according to the way in which
they produce sound, including aerophones, chordophones,
electrophones, idiophones, and membranophones.

ISBN 0–7910–5168–4 (hardcover)
1. Musical intruments—Juvenile literature. [1. Musical
instruments.] I. Title. II. Series.
ML460.H33 1998   98–36094
784.19—dc21   CIP
                                                  AC MN

CONTENTS

INTRODUCTION

For as long as people have known that other cultures existed, they have been curious about the differences in their customs and traditions. Julius Caesar, the famous Roman leader, wrote long chronicles about the inhabitants of Gaul (modern-day France) while he was leading troops in the Gallic Wars (58–51 B.C.). In the chronicles, he discussed their religious beliefs, their customs, their day-to-day life, and the conflicts among the different groups. Explorers like Marco Polo traveled thousands of miles and devoted years of their lives to learning about the peoples of the East and bringing home the stories of Chinese court life, along with the silks, spices, and inventions of that culture. The Chelsea House series *Costume, Tradition, and Culture: Reflecting on the Past* continues this legacy of exploration and discovery by discussing some of the most fascinating traditions, beliefs, legends, and artifacts from around the world.

Different cultures develop traditions and costumes to mark the roles of people in their societies, to commemorate events in their histories, and to make the changes and mysteries of life more meaningful. Soldiers wear uniforms to show that they are serving in their nation's army, and insignia on the uniforms show what ranks they hold within the army. People of Bukhara, a city in Uzbekistan, have for centuries woven fine threads of gold into their clothes, and when they travel to other cities they can be recognized as Bukharans by the golden embroidery on their traditional costume. For many years, in the Irish countryside, people would leave bowls of milk outside at night as an offering to the fairies, or "Good People," believing that this would help ensure their favor and keep the family safe from fairy mischief. In Mexico, November 2 is the Day of the Dead, when people visit cemeteries and have feasts to remember their ancestors. In the United States, brides wear white dresses, and the traditional wedding includes many rituals: the father of the bride "giving her away" to the groom, the exchange of vows and rings, the throwing of rice, the tossing of the bride's bouquet. These rituals and symbols help make the marriage meaningful and special for the couple, their families, and their friends, by expressing the change that is taking place and allowing the friends and families to wish luck to the couple.

This series will explore some of the myths, symbols, costumes, and traditions of various cultures from around the world and different times in the past. *Fighting Units of the American War of Independence,* for example, will detail the uniforms, weapons, and decorations of the regiments and battalions on both sides of the war, along with the battles in which they became famous. *Roman Myths, Heroes, and Legends* describes how the ancient Romans explained the wonders and natural phenomena of their world with fantastic stories of superhuman heroes and almost human deities who could change the course of history at will. In *Popular Superstitions,* you will learn how some familiar superstitious beliefs—such as throwing spilled salt over your shoulder, or hanging a horseshoe over your door for good luck—originally began, in times when people feared that devils and evil spirits were meddling in their lives. Few people still believe in malicious spirits, but many still toss the spilled salt over their shoulders, or knock on wood when expressing cautious hope. The legendary figures of a culture—the brave explorers of *The Wild West* or the wicked brigands described in *Infamous Pirates*— help shape that culture's values by providing grand, almost mythical examples of what people should (or should not!) strive to be.

The illustrations that accompany these books have their own cultural history. Originally, they were printed on small collectors' cards and sold in the early 20th century. Each card in a set of 25 or 50 would depict a different person, artifact, or event, and usually the reverse side would offer a few sentences of description to explain the picture. Now, they provide a fascinating glimpse into history and an entertaining addition to the stories presented here.

ABOUT THE AUTHOR

JUDY L. HASDAY, a native of Philadelphia, Pennsylvania, received her B.A. in communications and her Ed.M. in instructional technologies from Temple University. A multimedia professional, she has had her photographs published in several magazines and books, including a number of Chelsea House titles. She is also a freelance author of biographies for young adults, including *James Earl Jones* and *Madeleine Albright*.

OVERVIEW

Musical Instruments

M usic has been described as the universal language. No matter where you live or what kind of traditions or customs you follow, there are no barriers to prevent you from taking pleasure in music. Music inspires and motivates, enhances ceremonial and spiritual observances, and simply entertains. And there would be no music without instruments to create its sounds and rhythms.

When humans first banged sticks against rocks or fired arrows from hunting bows, they created different sounds and "tones." Petroglyphs—drawings and paintings found on cave walls and rocks—depict figures blowing on animal horns or shaking gourds, an early form of a rattle. The design of many of these early instruments suggests that they had a specific purpose other than pleasure. Blowing a horn or conch shell, for example, might alert others to impending danger or intimidate an enemy.

Initially, musical instruments were classified into two groups: those that were blown and those that were struck or plucked. In 1914 musicologists Curt Sachs and Erich Moritz von Hornbostel developed a system that categorized instruments by the way their sounds are produced. Aerophones, which produce sound by the vibration of air, include the saxophone, organ, and bagpipes. Chordophones, like the harp, guitar, violin, and piano, produce sounds by the vibration of strings.

Idiophones, like rattles, xylophones, and castanets, produce sounds when they are shaken or struck against another object. Membranophones, which produce sound when a stretched membrane or skin is struck, include drums such as the snare, timpani, barrel, and tom-tom. "Modern technology" instruments, or electrophones, include the electric guitar, vibraphone, and synthesizer.

ACCORDION

ost musical instruments are played as part of an orchestral ensemble or a concert band. However, a few are more suited to solo performance, and the accordion is such an instrument. Though it has what looks like a keyboard attached to one side, it is a free reed, bellows-operated wind instrument.

The accordion is a portable, hand-held instrument that consists of pleated bellows, a keyboard similar to that of a piano on one side, and buttons on the other. As the musician squeezes and pulls the pleated bellows back and forth with the left hand, he or she forces air through metal reeds inside the accordion. The forced air vibrates the reeds, which produce the musical sounds.

The accordion is constructed with two sets of reeds; one set vibrates when the bellows are pulled apart, the other when the player squeezes the bellows back together again. Operating this instrument in this fashion enables the musician to play any note, regardless of which direction the bellows are moving.

The right hand plays the melody on the vertical keyboard; the left hand, in addition to squeezing the bellows, fingers the buttons to play notes and chords, either singly or with several buttons depressed at the same time. The most important aspect of playing the accordion well is learning how to move the bellows back and forth smoothly, so the music is uninterrupted.

Primarily a folk instrument, the accordion is usually heard in dance halls, cafes, and on the streets. Myron Floren, probably the most recognized musician of the Lawrence Welk band, is considered the preeminent accordion player of the 20th century.

BAGPIPE

The bagpipe has a long and colorful history, from its probable origins in the Far East to its thriving popularity as the predominant musical instrument of Scotland. Though the bagpipe belongs to the wind instrument family, it is much more complex in design than its flute and recorder ancestors.

The bagpipe may have evolved when a bag made from a small animal skin was added to the aulos, a combination simple chanter and drone. The cylindrical or cone-shaped chanter is a reed pipe fitted with finger holes on which the melody is played. Drones are also fitted with reeds, but they have no holes, so they produce only a single note.

The bags can be made of leather or rubber and are inflated using either a bellows or a blowpipe. Sound is produced when the player squeezes the air from the inflated bag, forcing it up into the drones. Because the reeds vibrate from the air forced through the bag and not directly from the player's mouth, the musician can breathe while playing without interrupting the bagpipe's sound.

The most familiar bagpipe today is the mouth-blown plob-mhor, better known as the great Scottish Highland bagpipe. Its colorful tartan-covered bag and three large drones rest on the shoulder of the piper attired in full military dress; for centuries its distinctive discordant sound has accompanied Scottish regiments heading into battle. As the harbinger of war, the piper has always enjoyed a distinguished position within his clan.

The Lowland or Northumbrian bagpipe pictured is smaller that the Scottish Highland bagpipe and produces its stirring sounds through bellows that are fastened under the arm of the player.

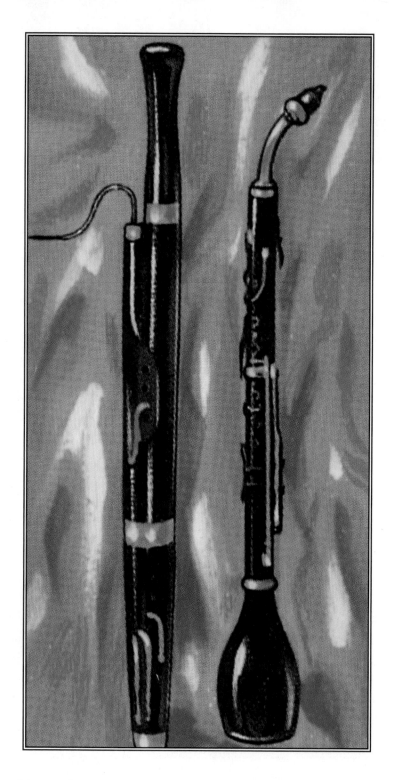

BASSOON AND BASSET HORN

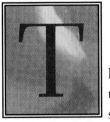

The bassoon and basset horn are members of the woodwind family. They function on the simple principle of their flute and panpipe ancestors: sound is produced when air, blown into the hollow tubelike instrument, vibrates. By adjusting the distance the air column travels, one determines the pitch (how high or low a musical note is). Woodwinds also have holes bored into them; when covered (by fingers or "keys"), these holes lengthen the air column, producing a lower note or deeper tone.

Woodwinds (with the exception of the flute) employ a reed mouthpiece to create air vibrations. Some, like the clarinet, use a single reed, while others, like the bassoon, have a double reed. The thin opening of a double reed limits the air flow so the musician can play a group of notes in one breath.

The bassoon, mainly an orchestral instrument, appeared sometime during the 17th century. Though it's not obvious when you look at the instrument, its wooden tube extends nine feet because two parallel tubes are joined at their lower ends to create a single U-shaped tube.

For ease of playing, the double reed is fitted into a curved tube called a crook. The lowest-sounding regular member of an orchestral wind section, the bassoon produces a pleasing mellow bass sound.

The basset horn, another double-reed woodwind, is a variation of the clarinet. Like the bassoon, it is primarily an orchestral wind instrument. Mozart wrote two parts for the basset horn in his well-known Requiem. Developed about 1770, the basset horn's early design included a curved wooden tube with a flared metal bell at its end. Today basset horns are similar in shape to the modern bass clarinet.

CORNET

The first horn instruments were made from animal horn. For example, the shofar, used by the Hebrews in biblical times, is made from a ram's horn. Today it is blown in synagogues during the Jewish High Holy Days. Over time, different materials such as wood and metal were employed in the design of horn instruments.

There are two families of wind instruments: woodwinds and brass. Many were originally used for hunting, herding flocks, and signaling messages. A woodwind instrument, however, produces air-vibrated sounds quite differently from the way brass instruments, such as the cornet and saxophone, create music. Brass instruments have valves that, when pressed down by the player's fingers, force the air in the tube to travel farther, producing a deeper note. Another major difference is in the mouthpieces: woodwinds have reeds, while brass instruments have cup-shaped metal mouthpieces.

The cornet is believed to have been invented by Jean-Louis Antoine in Paris, France, around 1828. Antoine conceived the idea of adding valves to the coiled post horn, a 15th-century instrument used by postmen to announce their arrival and departure. The cornet looks very much like the trumpet; however, its shorter body and a bore that widens past the valves before reaching the bell produces a "fatter," less piercing sound than the trumpet.

Long used in military and marching bands, the cornet's mellow, appealing sound is popular in jazz. Louis "Satchmo" Armstrong, remembered as one of the greatest trumpeters in jazz history, wowed audiences with his sizzling cornet solos as early as the 1920s.

FRENCH HORN

Like other brass wind instruments, including the cornet and tuba, the French horn was born out of a long tradition of signaling instruments found in ancient Greek and Roman civilizations. In France it was used mainly in hunting. Its use as a musical instrument, however, did not begin until the late 17th century.

It would be difficult to handle and play a 12-foot horn—the length the French horn would be if the looped and twisted tubing were straightened. The coiled shape conceals the fact that the French horn is actually two horns in one. And though it is a member of the brass wind instrument family, its double-horn design is not the only thing that distinguishes it from its brass counterparts.

The metal mouthpiece of the French horn is funnel shaped instead of cup shaped like that of the cornet and the tuba. And the French horn is fitted with rotary valves, added during the early 19th century, instead of piston valves. These are controlled by depressing the levers connected to them.

Within the French horn's unusual design, a small lever manipulated by the thumb shuts off one section of the tubing. Switching between the two sets of tubing allows the musician to play brilliant high notes from the shorter tubing and warm, low notes from the longer tubing.

The player can also manipulate sound by inserting the right hand into the flared bell. Partially closing off the throat of the bell flattens the tone, and closing it off tightly creates a muting effect. The French horn has the widest range of notes of all the brass and woodwinds, making it an essential musical instrument for any orchestra.

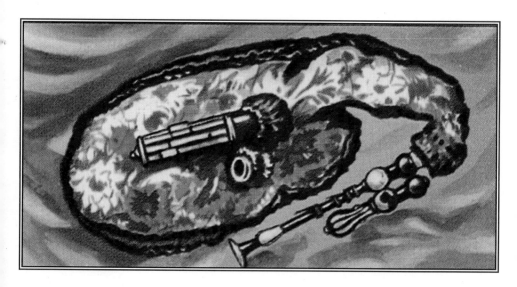

MUSETTE

The earliest documentation of the bagpipe dates from the first century A.D., although it is possible that the instrument is much older, since mouth-blown reed pipes are more than 3,000 years old. Ancient cultures in India or the Middle East could conceivably have attached an animal-skin bag to a musical pipe to create a primitive version of this plaintive-sounding wind instrument.

We do know, however, that the first mention of the bagpipe identifies the Roman emperor Nero as a piper. Most historians believe that the instrument was introduced to western Europe—including England, Ireland, and Scotland—by the Romans.

Various forms of the bagpipe exist in different regions of the world. Some are mouth-blown; others are bellows-blown. Some have single reed chanters, others have three drones. The most recognized is the Scottish Highland bagpipe, a large mouth-blown bagpipe.

The French musette is a smaller bagpipe—similar to the Scottish Lowland bagpipe or the Irish uilleann pipe—and employs bellows located under the piper's arm to inflate the bag.

Popular in European aristocratic circles in the 17th and 18th centuries, the softly toned musette was lavishly adorned. Its two double-reed chanters with silver keys (for semitones) and its set of four to six double-reed drones were made of ebony and ivory instead of wood or bone. The bags were finished in silk or velvet with intricate embroidery work, and the small bellows were crafted of walnut inlaid with pieces of wood, shell, or ivory in a detailed design.

OLIPHANT

Animal bones and horns were among the earliest materials used to create musical instruments. After the marrow was removed and the bone was suitably dried, early musicians cut holes into the bone at intervals along its length. When players blew into the instrument, the resulting sounds varied in pitch depending on which holes were covered by their fingers. This type of instrument was the predecessor of the flute and the recorder.

By the Middle Ages, people were using animal horns mostly as signaling instruments for hunting and herding flocks rather than for creating music. Ivory tusks were particularly prized, because when the end was chipped off and one blew into it, the sound that was produced imitated the bellow of the elephant, which was viewed as a symbol of power and strength. Medieval soldiers blew these horns in an attempt to strike fear into the hearts of their enemies just before engaging in battle.

Oliphants, as these ivory horns became known, were first made during the 10th and 11th centuries. Finely carved and often elaborately adorned with silverwork or other metals, they were crafted mostly by Muslims in southern Italy and on the island of Sicily.

Unlike other horns of the times, oliphants were also fitted with metal bands with loops to accommodate the attachment of a slinging chain or strap for carrying. Over the centuries, this horn evolved into a metal construction with special fitted mouthpieces. By the 18th century, the oliphant had become an accepted orchestral musical instrument. The one pictured here is approximately 28 inches long and is believed to be from the early 16th century.

PORTABLE ORGAN

nvented over 2,000 years ago, the organ is the most ancient of all keyboard musical instruments and the most unusual. While the strings of a piano are struck and the strings of a harpsichord are plucked, the organ's sound is produced when compressed air flows along its pipes.

The technical, mechanical, and visual intricacies of the organ make it one of the most impressive musical instruments ever designed. Its most striking feature is the rows of graduated, flutelike pipes. But many of the individual parts of this complex instrument—which include keys and a wind mechanism that helps produce sound—are not visible to the observer.

The origins of the organ can be traced to the simple panpipe. According to legend, the Greek god Pan was in love with a water nymph, who was turned into a reed while escaping his advances. Using this reed, Pan created a wind instrument which he played to console himself over her loss. The organ's pipe design comes from the arrangement of the panpipe's flutes of graduated sizes; in the panpipe, they are joined together and played by blowing air across the tops of the holes.

During the late Middle Ages, the portable organ, used primarily as a procession instrument, was designed to be carried or placed on a table. It was slung by a strap over the player's shoulder so that the bellows could be operated by the left hand and the keys by the right hand. Some music composed for the portable organ during the Renaissance still survives. The music played by the portable organ has been described as "so beautiful that even the birds listen to it."

SAXOPHONE

O f all the woodwind instruments, the saxophone is the most modern and probably the most recognizable to nonmusicians. Most present-day musical instrument designs are the result of years—in some cases centuries—of development. However, the saxophone has not changed since it was invented by the Belgian-born instrument maker Adolphe Sax in the early 1840s.

In an effort to create an instrument that would amplify the sound produced by the woodwinds in military bands, Sax experimented by attaching the reeded clarinet mouthpiece to a brass horn. The new sound produced when he blew into it was more powerful than ordinary woodwinds but retained their rich, mellow, and familiar tones. He added keys to the design and was granted a patent in 1846.

Because most orchestral music was composed before the saxophone was invented, few compositions include parts written for this hybrid instrument. However, late 19th-century composers eventually began incorporating the saxophone into orchestral pieces, such as the hauntingly passionate *Bolero* by French composer Maurice Ravel.

The advent of jazz in the 20th century created a demand for the sound of this unique instrument in a way that Adolphe Sax could not have imagined. The saxophone's broad range of tonalities, achieved by varying mouthpiece, reed, and lip-and-tongue playing techniques, produces a powerfully expressive sound that has played the lead role in jazz. Charlie Parker was arguably the finest jazz saxophonist. His brilliant technique heavily influenced jazz saxophone greats such as John Coltrane, Gerry Mulligan, and David Sanborn.

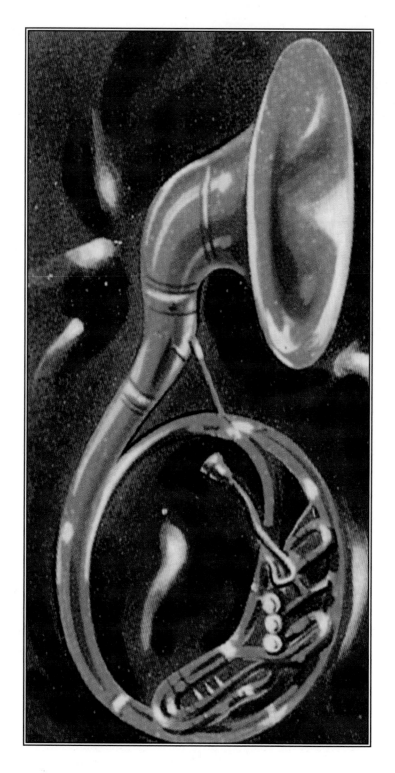

SOUSAPHONE

The sousaphone, one of the largest brass instruments in the horn family, was named after American bandmaster and composer John Philip Sousa and is used primarily in marching bands. Sousa, best known for composing such anthems as "Stars and Stripes Forever" and "Semper Fidelis," suggested the design to J. W. Pepper, a Philadelphia music teacher and merchant.

With the help of instrument-maker John Distin, Pepper had begun manufacturing musical instruments around 1880. Their first sousaphone model, created in 1892, was fashioned after another large brass instrument, the tubalike helicon, crafted in Vienna, Austria, about 40 years earlier.

The name "helicon" comes from the instrument's helical design. The tubing encircles the musician's body, while the instrument rests on the left shoulder and passes under the right arm, with the bell above the musician's head.

At first the enormous bell of the sousaphone pointed straight up, earning the nickname "the rain catcher." In describing the instrument's unusual design, Sousa said it "projected the sound upward and mushroomed it over the entire band and audience." In 1908 the C. G. Conn Company of Elkhart, Indiana, modified the design by tilting the bell forward. In recent years the bell has also been constructed out of fiberglass to reduce the instrument's overall weight.

The sousaphone's low, robust tone and physical enormity distinguish it from other large brass instruments. You are most likely to see and hear the sousaphone during a marching band performance at halftime ceremonies at a football game, or in holiday parades.

TUBA

he tuba is the largest of the brass wind instruments. Its massive size and extensive coiled tubing require strong lips and lungs to blow through the cup-shaped mouthpiece. With its wide, cone-shaped bore design and large flaring bell, the tuba is most known for the deep, rich tones it produces.

Despite its cumbersome appearance, however, the tuba is a versatile instrument, capable of producing a much broader musical range than the "oom-pah-pah" orchestral accompaniment it is most often associated with.

The Romans coined the name "tuba" to describe the brass instrument that was the predecessor of the trumpet. About four feet long and played with a detachable bone mouthpiece, the Roman tuba was primarily sounded to accompany marching or to signal an attack or retreat in battle. As such, it functioned more as a means of communication than as an accompanying instrument in musical performances.

Over time this simple brass tube was redesigned and renamed hundreds of times. To some extent, all cup mouthpiece horns in use today can be traced back to the Roman ancestor of the tuba.

The present shape and function of the large tubas used in orchestras and jazz ensembles were invented in Berlin, Germany, around 1835, for use in military bands. Basically a huge upright valved bugle, the modern tuba comes in five sizes, ranging from the euphonium (the word derives from the Greek *euphonia* meaning "well-sounding") to the contrabass tuba. The largest tuba, measuring 8 feet in height, would stretch out more than 45 feet in length if uncoiled.

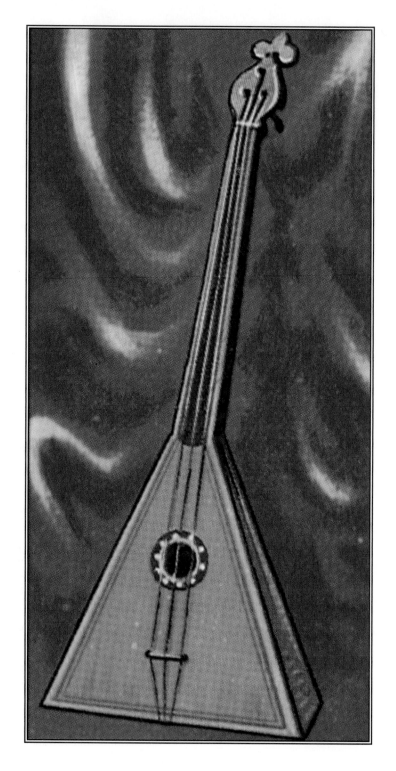

BALALAIKA

Each country has its own musical style, characterized by traditional instruments reflecting a wide range of influences. For example, African music, often an important element in ceremonies and rituals, is dominated by the powerful, percussive beat of drums.

The music of Russia and the Slavic region is equally distinctive—its sounds distinguished by many varieties of stringed musical instruments, such as the fiddle, harp, and lute. These instruments are particularly popular among folk musicians—everyday people who compose and play songs about daily life. Folk songs often tell a story, either imaginary or real, that reflect their culture's customs and traditions. Learned by listening and playing, folk music is passed from one generation to the next over centuries.

The distinctive sound of Russian folk music is synonymous with the balalaika, a three-stringed, long-necked lute with an unusual triangular body. It is plucked with the fingers. It is believed to have been invented by the Tartar tribes of Russia around 1700. A descendant of the dombra, the balalaika has also long been a favorite folk instrument among the gypsies, who play it to accompany songs and dances.

The balalaika's sound is often described as melancholy. In Europe it was primarily played as a solo instrument, much like the guitar. Because the balalaika is made in six sizes, from the small piccolo to the large double bass, it is also well suited for ensemble performance. In recent years, balalaika orchestras have become popular in Russia and elsewhere.

LUTE

he lute, among the oldest plucked-string instruments, has been pictured on Mesopotamian pottery dating from 2000 B.C. It is actually a descendant of both the Arabic ud, which came from Africa, and the pandoura, which was found in Greece and Rome.

The ud (meaning "wood") was first introduced into Europe by the Moors during their conquest of Spain in A.D. 711. Unlike other stringed instruments of the period, which were often made from a single gourd, the ud was constructed from separate wooden segments.

Though the reasons for the name change are unclear, by the 15th century the ud became known as the lute. By plucking the strings with a plectrum (a pick) or the fingers, the lute created lovely sounds and became a popular musical instrument during the Renaissance period.

Lutes come in a variety of styles and sizes and can be found on almost every continent in the world. The lute is built with only wood and glue; no nails or screws are used in its construction. The 17th-century Italian lute pictured here has a half-pear-shaped, rounded body, built on wooden ribs that were curved by a steaming process; an ornate soundhole and flat top; and a short, fretted neck with the pegbox bent back nearly 90 degrees, fitted with 20 strings that run from the pegbox to the bridge of the instrument.

A bass form of the lute, called a theorbo, has a neck several feet long to allow especially deep tones.

The lute is often mentioned in English literature, including Shakespeare's poem "The Passionate Pilgrim," and is depicted being played by angels in many Renaissance paintings, such as Rosso Fiorentino's *Angel Musician* (c. 1519).

MOON GUITAR

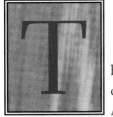

The classical music of China has had a significant influence on the countries of Southeast Asia. These musical traditions go back thousands of years. About the time that music was beginning to take organized form in Europe, China had already developed a complete musical theory system and several advanced musical instruments.

Much of the credit goes to Confucius, who advocated the practice of orthodox ritual music. During the Han Dynasty (206 B.C. to A.D. 220), a Music Bureau was established by China's imperial court to oversee the acquisition and editing of ancient music and folk songs.

Around this time, a variation of the lute, called the p'i-p'a, and a vertically held violin, the hu-ch'in, were introduced to the Chinese. Some time in the mid-eighth century A.D., the Pear Garden Academy song and dance troupe was created, attracting a large number of musicians and establishing a firm foundation for Chinese music.

Traditional Chinese music has a distinctive rhythm, beat, and tonal quality. This is mainly due to the sounds and playing styles of the instruments used. The more unusual instruments include spike fiddles, gongs, panpipes, and lutes.

Many types of lutes exist in almost every part of the world. The yueh-ch'in, pictured here, is a short-necked, flat, round-bodied lute that was invented during the Chin Dynasty (A.D. 265–420). It is often called the moon guitar of China because of the shape of its soundboard. Strung with four silk strings over 10 frets that extend well past the neck and onto the body, the yueh-ch'in is used primarily to accompany voice performances and is often part of Chinese opera ensembles.

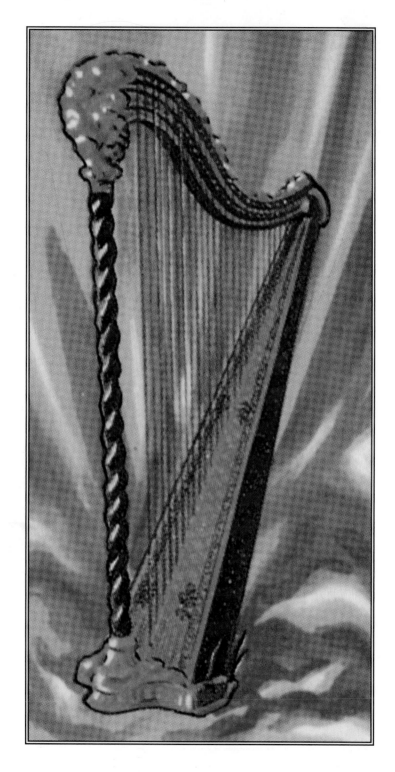

PEDAL HARP

The harp is the oldest of all stringed instruments. The delicate but full-bodied resonance produced by plucking the strings sounds far more beautiful than the instrument that inspired its creation, the primitive one-stringed musical bow.

Stringed instruments were played by the ancient Greeks and Egyptians. The Greek philosopher Pythagoras discovered that the pitch created by plucking a stretched string is related to the string's length: the longer the string, the lower the note. Because these early instruments were designed with few strings, they could produce no more than a few musical notes. Adding more strings made the harp too large and too difficult to play.

When a pedal mechanism was added, much like that of the piano, the harpist was able to play a greater range of notes. The number of pedals varied, until the 19th-century French piano maker Sebastian Erard standardized the harp's design by setting the pedal number at seven, equaling the notes in the musical scale.

Grand orchestral pedal harps are about 6 feet tall and weigh 85–90 pounds. The 47 strings, which cover six octaves, are color-coded—C strings are red and F strings are blue or black—making it easier for the musician to see them. The harpist uses both feet to press the seven pedals—three on the left and four on the right.

Today the sounds created by plucking the 47 strings of the modern orchestral pedal harp are often described as "heavenly." Throughout history, the harp has been strongly associated with a sense of righteousness and virtue. The harp seems ever-present in religious paintings. Artists often show it being played by angels.

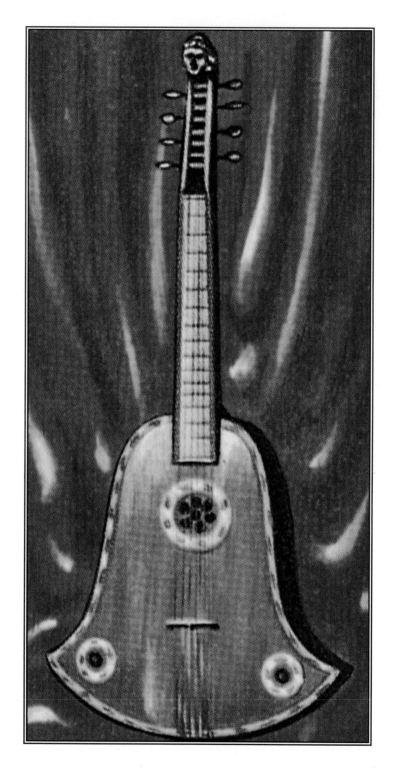

QUINTERNA

The quinterna, popular during the 16th and 17th centuries, was also known as the Italian guitar. Like most modern plucked-string instruments, it was a descendent of the lute. Though made in many different shapes and sizes, all lutes shared the common characteristics of a resonating belly, a neck, and strings running from near the base of the belly along the full length of the neck.

Different types of lutes are distinguished by the length of the neck and body, the shape of the back of the instrument, the number of strings, and whether or not there are frets, or ridges, fixed across the fingerboards. The style of the lute's back indicates its age and origin. A round-backed lute, for example, was typical of Renaissance Europe, while the flat-backed lute resembled the European classical guitar.

The quinterna was a member of the cittern family, one of the many groups of plucked-string instruments that descended from the guitar. Because citterns were easy to play and less expensive than lutes, they were popular instruments among amateur musicians.

The flat-backed, bell-shaped body of the quinterna pictured here is made of tortoise shell and adorned with decorative ivory accents. It has three pairs of catgut strings and two single wire-covered strings, and the neck terminates in a hand-carved ornamental head figure. Once widely played by Italian peasants, the quinterna, like many other citterns, waned in popularity by the 19th century and was set aside in favor of the guitar.

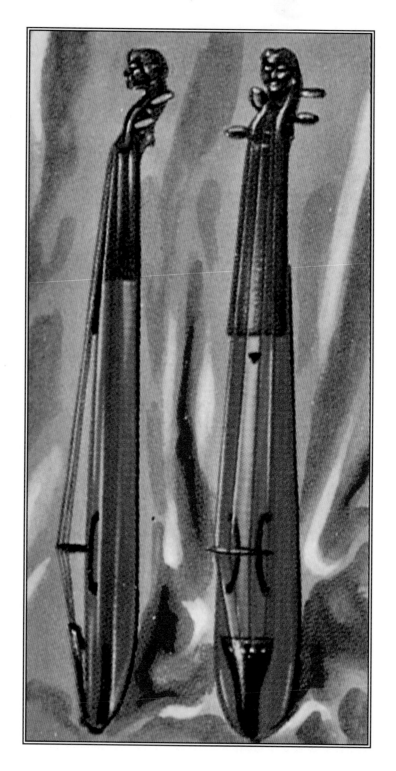

SORDINO

tringed instruments are plucked, struck, or bowed to set the strings vibrating and create sound. Modern stringed instruments are the culmination of centuries of experimentation, modification, and development. For example, both guitars and violins have been crafted from various hardwoods and fitted with different string materials such as silk, animal gut, and metal in the quest to produce the best sound.

By the Middle Ages, the stringed instruments most often depicted in paintings were played in one of two ways: either positioned on the arm or shoulder, like the violin, or standing upright like the viol (an early form of the cello).

Throughout history, stringed instruments have varied as much in style and design as in the sounds they produce and in how they are played. One such instrument, the 16th-century kit violin, evolved from the rebec, another ancestor of the violin. This instrument, which is called the sordino in Italian and the pochette—literally meaning "pocket"—in French, is actually a miniature violin, so small that it fit into the pocket of a man's coat, thus earning the nickname "pocket fiddle."

The sordino remained popular for about 200 years, especially among dance masters and street musicians. Dance masters not only had to direct their pupils in their steps, they also had to supply the music. So although the sordino didn't produce a particularly beautiful sound from its very narrow soundbox, it was a handy instrument because its convenient size made it easily retrievable for music lessons.

SPANISH GUITAR

One of the most popular stringed instruments played today is the acoustic or "Spanish" guitar. Like many other present-day stringed instruments, such as the violin and the harp, the guitar's ancestry can be traced back thousands of years.

The name "guitar" comes from the Greek *kithara*, a type of lyre. Most historians believe the guitar was introduced to Spain by the Arabs. Because of its plucking and strumming versatility, it quickly became an established musical instrument throughout Europe.

The guitar we know today went through various stages of development. Prior to the 1800s it was smaller and narrower than the present-day style. In 1863 Antonio de Torres, who is considered the father of the modern acoustic guitar, experimented with different designs and constructions in an effort to improve its overall sound and volume. He set the string length at 650 millimeters, which naturally determined the size and proportions of the figure-eight-shaped body and the length of the fingerboard.

The basic chord and strumming style can be simple to learn, which is one reason the guitar is such a popular instrument. However, learning the complex finger-picking techniques for playing classical compositions or bluegrass can take years to master.

In the 20th century, the Spanish virtuoso guitarist Andres Segovia established the guitar as a serious concert instrument. Largely self-taught, Segovia fell in love with the guitar when he was a boy, learning everything he could about its art, history, and design. His stunning performances throughout Europe and America earned the guitar a respected place in modern concert halls worldwide.

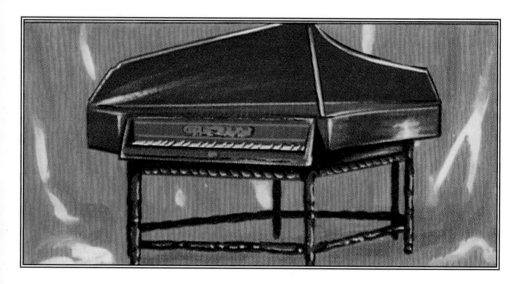

SPINET

The spinet may look like a miniature version of a grand piano, but it produces sounds in a different way. In the piano, the strings are struck percussively by rebounding hammers, resulting in a smooth, mellow tone. The spinet, whose strings are plucked mechanically, has a more metallic, tinny sound. The spinet's music is closely related to other keyboard instruments of the Renaissance and Baroque periods.

The clavichord, harpsichord, virginal, and spinet were probably designed as attempts to find a method of playing a series of strings in a way other than plucking or strumming them by hand. The answer came in the 15th century with the advent of the keyboard, which had long been used to sound the sets of pipes in organs. Combining string instruments with keyboards created a whole new way to produce sound.

Mechanically, these instruments all produce their sounds in the same way. Only the arrangement of strings makes them different from one another. For example, in virginals, the strings run parallel to the keyboard; in the spinet, however, they run off diagonally to the right. Basically, the player presses a key, which raises a wooden jack with a leather wedge (called a pick) or a quill that plucks the string. The spinet's name may have come from the Latin word *spinae,* meaning "thorns," a reference to the shape of those tiny quills.

Because the spinet was smaller and less expensive than its keyboard counterparts, it became very popular during the late 17th and 18th centuries, particularly in England. The spinet pictured here is a late-17th-century model manufactured on Threadneedle Street in London by a famous spinet maker, Stephen Keane.

UPRIGHT SPINET

he Renaissance period, which reached its height in the 15th and 16th centuries, was characterized by a "rebirth" of art, music, and learning. It began in Italy in the 1300s, and over the next 200 years spread throughout the rest of Europe. It was a time of great intellectual awakening, as people began to challenge existing beliefs and explore a world beyond their own towns and villages.

By the 1600s sculpture, painting, and architecture had begun to communicate the dynamic and emotionally expressive energy of their creators. The breathtaking work of composers such as Johann Sebastian Bach highlighted the contrasts between loud and soft music and between slow and quick tempos. Dramatic performances became married to music, giving birth to the opera.

The most important keyboard instrument of the Baroque period, which began at the end of the Renaissance, was the harpsichord. It was popular among composers because of its bright, clear sound. Other varieties, like the virginal and the spinet, came later. Both are smaller than the harpsichord and were designed primarily for use in the home.

In the late 15th century, a very unusual spinet style was invented. The upright spinet—quite literally a spinet mounted vertically—was designed to take up less space. For example, the one pictured here, only two feet wide, is five feet tall. The most striking feature of the upright spinet and its relatives is their ornately decorated cases, many of which have detailed pastoral scenes painted on their lids and bodies.

ELECTRIC
GUITAR

The electric guitar was created during the explosion of 20th-century innovations in music. It is the driving force behind rock 'n' roll music. And though the electric guitar physically resembles the acoustic (or Spanish) guitar, the similarity ends there.

The acoustic guitar has a hollow body that functions like an echo chamber, resonating with the sound the strings make when plucked. The only way to increase the volume of an acoustic guitar is to attach a microphone that is plugged into an amplifier.

When the electric guitar is played, however, the string vibrations do not echo in a hollow chamber, instead, the sounds are translated into electrical impulses by a magnetized device called a "pickup." The field produced by the pickup varies depending on the specific vibration. These altered electrical signals travel through an amplifier, which modifies the impulses before they are emitted from a speaker that translates the impulses back into sounds. For special sound effects, a player may employ other devices, such as the "wah-wah" pedal and the tremolo arm.

Pioneering designers of the electric guitar include the Gibson Company, which first fitted a Spanish guitar with a single pickup in 1935. Leo Fender built the first solid-body electric guitar and produced the famous Stratocaster in 1954.

Of the great contemporary electric guitarists—including Chuck Berry, Bo Diddley, and Eric Clapton—Jimi Hendrix had the most unusual playing technique. A natural left-hander, he played a right-handed guitar upside down, with the controls at the top and the strings in reverse sequence.

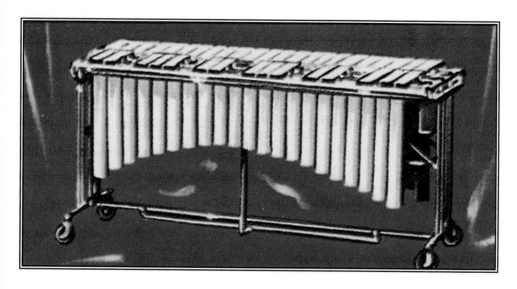

VIBRAPHONE

member of the percussion family of instruments, the vibraphone, originally called a vibraharp, was invented in 1910 in the United States. It is a descendant of similar musical instruments, such as the xylophone, found in Africa; the marimba, found in Latin America; and the gamelan orchestral instruments of Bali and Java in Southeast Asia.

Probably the most well known of this family is the xylophone, which derives its name from the Greek *xylon,* meaning wood, and *phonein,* meaning sound. It is constructed of wooden bars of different lengths arranged by tone and mounted on a frame. Resonators, often made from the calabash gourd, are attached underneath the bars.

The marimba looks like the xylophone, but instead of being fitted with calabash resonators, it has pipes of varying lengths corresponding to the pitch of the respective tone bars. The metallophones popular with gamelan orchestras also resemble the xylophone, but their bars are made of metal rather than wood.

The vibraphone has metal bars arranged in keyboard fashion and is fitted with special resonators that can be electronically amplified. When the bars are struck with mallets, the vibraphone produces a pulsating tone called vibrato, created when the upper ends of the resonators are opened and closed by revolving, motor-driven, metal discs called vanes. When no vibrato is desired, the vanes sit in the vertical position, with the resonators open.

The vibraphone has been a favorite instrument among jazz musicians. Lionel Hampton, the undisputed "King of the Vibraphone," began playing the vibes in the 1930s while recording with jazz trumpeter Louis Armstrong.

RANAT

usical instruments are as diverse and unique as the peoples of the cultures who play them. One region of the world, Southeast Asia—comprising countries such as Thailand, Myanmar, Cambodia, Malaysia, and the many islands of Indonesia—has a long history of using musical instruments to accompany dancing, religious ceremonies, and battles. Percussion instruments have often been used in ritual ceremonies to chase away evil spirits or to please the gods.

Perhaps the most beautiful ceremonial music of all is performed by the gamelan orchestras of Java and Bali in Indonesia. These orchestras are composed primarily of instruments in the percussion family—drums, gongs, ranats, and chimes.

Ranats, Thai-style metallophones and xylophones, have two distinctive designs: in one style, the keys are metal bars (metallophones); in the other, they are bars crafted of wood or bamboo (xylophones).

The ranat ek, like the one pictured, consists of a hollowed-out sound box that rests on a pyramid-shaped pedestal. Twenty-one keys are strung on one cord through holes at the end of each key and then suspended about an inch above the sound box from four hooks at either end.

Varying in length from 12 inches to 15 inches, the keys are individually tuned to the musical scale and then fine-tuned by applying a mixture of melted beeswax and metal shavings to the underside of the keys' ends. Ranats are played with a pair of padded (for indoor use) or hard-knobbed (for outdoor use) beaters.

Drum Ensemble

rums have been around for thousands of years and come in hundreds of styles and shapes, ranging from the powerful orchestral timpani kettledrums to rhythmic Caribbean steel drums. The sounds of 20th-century music styles such as jazz and rock 'n' roll most often are accompanied by a group of drums and other percussion instruments known as a drum ensemble or "set."

Apart from the sheer physical energy that goes into playing a drum set, the ensemble musician must have the coordination to play several instruments at once. A typical drum set includes a bass drum, two to three bass-mounted tom-toms, a floor tom-tom, a snare drum, and three cymbals. Because the ensemble includes a variety of percussion instruments, the player can produce a wide range of sounds.

The bass drum lies on its side, and the drummer "thumps" it by stepping on a foot pedal connected to a felt-covered beater. Bass mounted tom-toms are smaller than the other drums, and they produce higher, more mellow notes when struck. The floor tom-tom, which is struck with mallets or the drummer's hands, produces deep, vibrant notes.

The snare drum is fitted with a set of taut wires across its base. When the player strikes the drum, these wires—the snare—vibrate against the drum's skin, producing a sharp "crack." Cymbals produce a clashing metallic sound.

Drum players use sticks, hard or soft mallets, and wire brushes to produce different sound effects. The striking motion may be easy to learn, but it is difficult to master. One of the world's great jazz drummers, Buddy Rich, struck his first set of drums at the tender age of 18 months.

INDIAN BARREL DRUM

rums are among the oldest musical instruments known to man. Since the beginning of civilization, the pounding sounds reverberating from drums have signaled messages ranging from alerting warriors to clashes with the enemy to sending bulletins over long distances.

Believing that drums have magical significance, many cultures made them an essential part of their ceremonial rituals. The rhythm of a drum is the pulse that drives music as diverse as a Japanese processional or a rock 'n' roll concert.

Whatever their use, the sound of drums has a powerful impact on the listener.

Drums produce sound when a membrane or skin stretched tightly over a cylinder-type frame is struck, creating a vibration. There are four ways of attaching skins to a drum: They may be glued, nailed, pegged, or laced. Lacing styles, like the N, W, and X patterns, provide a way to "dress up" the look of the drum. Made in dozens of styles and sizes, drums are usually categorized by their shape.

The Indian drum shown here is a double-headed barrel drum, meaning that skins are attached at both ends of the cylinder; Japanese daiko drums have a similar construction. Though this type of Indian drum is not used by professional musicians, it is often employed in small informal instrumental groups because of its simple rhythm.

As in the case of the Nautch dance, an Indian classical dance in which every movement and gesture tells a story of the Hindu gods and heroes, the Indian drum is used purely for its rhythmic accompaniment. A different type of drum, the tabla, which has only one skin, is played in Indian classical music.

CHRONOLOGY

30,000 years ago	First musical bows, gourd rattles, and bone flutes developed.
3500 B.C.	Emergence of the first civilization in Sumeria.
1000 B.C.	First mouth organ used in China.
200–100 B.C.	Flutes and panpipes played in the Andes, South America.
A.D. 500	Gongs first used in China.
10th–11th centuries	Oliphants crafted by Muslim artisans in southern Italy and Sicily.
11th century	Guido d'Arezza, a Benedictine monk, invents musical staff notation.
13th century	Sitar invented in India.
1350	Clavichord, early keyboard instrument, invented.
17th century	Stephen Keane invents the spinet.
18th century	Piano, sordino, basset horn invented.
1720	First petal mechanism invented for the harp, allowing changes of key.
19th century	Evolution of the small horn into other brass wind instruments including the cornet.
1820	First accordion invented; the keyboard was added later.

1829   Accordion patented.

1835   Tuba invented.

1846   Adolph Sax invents the saxophone.

1892   J. W. Pepper Company creates the sousaphone, named after marching band leader John Philip Sousa.

20th century   Vibraphone, electric guitar, synthesizers created as part of a wave of modern technology instruments.

INDEX ❦

FURTHER READING

Ardley, Neil. *Eyewitness Books: Music.* New York: Alfred A. Knopf, 1989.

Barber, Nicky, et al. *The Kingfisher Young People's Book of Music.* New York: Larousse Kingfisher Chambers, 1996.

Dearling, Robert, ed. *The Encyclopedia of Musical Instruments.* London: Carlton Books, 1996.

Diagram Group. *Musical Instruments of the World.* New York: Sterling Publishing Company, 1971.

Gottlieb, William P. *The Golden Age of Jazz.* New York: Da Capo Press, 1979.

Levine, Jack and Takeru Iijima. *Understanding Musical Instruments: How to Select Your Instrument.* New York: Frederick Warne, 1971.

Rademacher, Johannes. *Musical Instruments: An Illustrated Historical View.* New York: Barrons, 1997.